The Royal Estates
of
Britain

Photographs by
Earl A. Beesley and Garry Gibbons

Text by
Delia Millar

HARRY N. ABRAMS, INC., PUBLISHERS, NEW YORK

This book has been made possible by the Gracious Permission of Her Majesty The Queen, to whom we are deeply indebted for allowing us the privilege of free access to photograph the royal estates.
We also wish to thank Her Majesty for allowing us to reproduce paintings from the Royal Collection and a photograph from the Royal Photograph Collection.

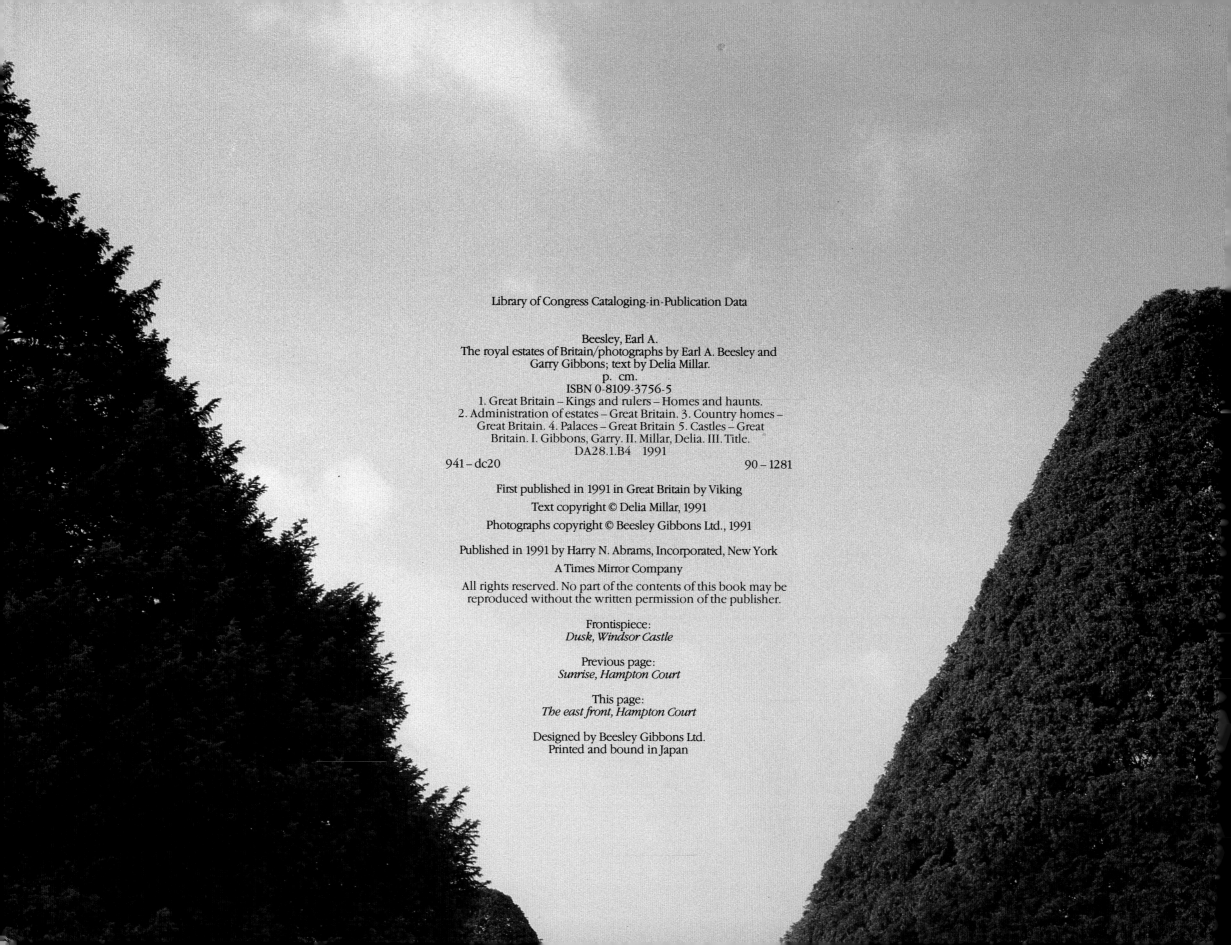

Library of Congress Cataloging-in-Publication Data

Beesley, Earl A.
The royal estates of Britain/photographs by Earl A. Beesley and
Garry Gibbons; text by Delia Millar.
p. cm.
ISBN 0-8109-3756-5
1. Great Britain – Kings and rulers – Homes and haunts.
2. Administration of estates – Great Britain. 3. Country homes –
Great Britain. 4. Palaces – Great Britain 5. Castles – Great
Britain. I. Gibbons, Garry. II. Millar, Delia. III. Title.
DA28.1.B4   1991
941–dc20   90–1281

First published in 1991 in Great Britain by Viking

Text copyright © Delia Millar, 1991

Photographs copyright © Beesley Gibbons Ltd., 1991

Published in 1991 by Harry N. Abrams, Incorporated, New York

A Times Mirror Company

Frontispiece:
Dusk, Windsor Castle

Previous page:
Sunrise, Hampton Court

This page:
The east front, Hampton Court

Designed by Beesley Gibbons Ltd.
Printed and bound in Japan

Contents

Foreword

Since the Norman Conquest, Britain's Royal Families have been linked with particular residences: we associate Henry VIII with Hampton Court, Queen Victoria and Prince Albert with Balmoral, Mary, Queen of Scots with the Palace of Holyroodhouse. The estates shown in this book span over 900 years of British royal history, from William the Conqueror, who laid the foundations for Windsor Castle, to our present Queen Elizabeth II.

The royal residences have a unique appeal: they are not only homes but something much more. They share a feeling of history and heritage, while at the same time reminding us that they have at some time in their lives been *family* homes, rebuilt, refurnished and adapted to suit the needs of their occupants as well as the requirements of State.

In preparing this book we were greatly privileged to be allowed access to the estates at all times. Our aim was to take the reader on a visual journey to show Britain's royal properties in a new light. We have photographed the buildings and their surroundings throughout the seasons, in the soft morning and evening light and in extremely dramatic weather, and more often than not under very difficult circumstances.

The weather was not always on our side. At 'dear old Sandringham', as King George V called it, harvesting was in progress in brilliant sunshine, and we saw the house at its best. At Hampton Court, however, where we were already restricted by the restoration work, the drought of the summer of 1989 turned the lawns parched and brown. At Edinburgh, to which we made nine journeys in all to photograph the Palace of Holyroodhouse, hours were spent waiting for the rain to stop before we could start work, and at Balmoral we had to wait until February for the snow, which in every other year starts to fall at Christmas.

Balmoral, Windsor and Sandringham are vast estates compared with Holyroodhouse and Buckingham Palace. The latter two are similar in that each is situated in the middle of a great city, yet we were struck by the feeling of peace and tranquility in the grounds of these two palaces. All the estates are natural reserves for animals, wildfowl and birds of many species, and we were surprised at the abundance of unusual wildlife, especially in the grounds of Buckingham Palace.

We were received with the same friendliness and helpfulness in all the areas of the country we travelled to – Scotland, Norfolk, Berkshire, Surrey and the heart of London – making the production of this book an experience we shall not forget.

Earl A. Beesley
Garry Gibbons

The Palace of Holyroodhouse, *painted in watercolour by James Duffield Harding for Queen Victoria.*

PALACE OF HOLYROODHOUSE

A mile east of Edinburgh Castle, at the foot of the Royal Mile, lies the Palace of Holyroodhouse, against the background of the grey rock and green turf of Arthur's Seat. The history of the palace, its bloodshed and dramas, still fascinates the modern visitor to this calm and handsome building.

'A jewel in architecture', the Palace of Holyroodhouse stands outside the town walls of Edinburgh, under the splendid heights of Arthur's Seat, 'in a park of Hares, Conies and Deare' as described by a sixteenth-century writer. Today it is enjoyed and used for many important functions, but for long periods in the past it was more like the palace of the Sleeping Beauty.

Holyrood was founded over 850 years ago as a community of Augustinian canons by David I, the 'paragon of all his kin'. The last surviving son of Malcolm III and his English Queen, King David was brought up in England, where 'he peeled off the rust of Scottish barbarism' and was, in the words of Sir Walter Scott, 'a wise, religious, and powerful prince'. Besides establishing the monastic house at Holyrood he 'founded bishopricks, and built and endowed many monasteries, which he vested with large grants of lands out of the patrimony of the kings'. With lavish assistance to the monastic houses of Kelso, Melrose, Kinloss, Jedburgh, Newbattle and others, he helped to build up the structure of Anglo-Norman culture in his kingdom. At Holyrood the canons erected a simple aisleless cruciform church, much enlarged in about 1220, of which the only surviving part is the processional doorway which led into the choir. David I founded the royal burgh of Edinburgh in about 1130, and the canons of Holyrood were permitted to found their own burgh in 1140. These new towns attracted merchants and craftsmen and helped to develop the trade of Edinburgh. The King's wisdom as a ruler was praised by his friend and panegyrist, Ailred, who wrote: 'Forgetting their natural roughness the Scots accepted with patient submission the laws his royal beneficence ordained.' The abbey foundation survived English attacks in the fourteenth century and sacking in the sixteenth century, but in 1569 the east end of the abbey church was destroyed by the Reformers, leaving only the nave, which survived because it was being used as a parish church by the inhabitants of Canongate.

From the early fifteenth century Holyrood had been a royal residence. James IV added a large north-west tower to the late medieval building and in 1503 celebrated his marriage there to the fifteen-year-old Margaret Tudor, daughter of Henry VII. By this union 'an end was put to all future national wars, by their great-grandson, James VI of Scotland and I of England, becoming King of the whole island of Great Britain'. James IV met his bride six miles from Edinburgh at Newbattle Abbey and rode to Holyrood upon the same horse, to be greeted by tournaments, tilts and various entertainments in honour of the occasion. In one of these the King, wearing wild dress as the 'Savage Knight', took part in such life-like fights with Highland chieftains that several of the participants were actually wounded.

The building of Holyroodhouse was completed in the reign of his son James V, and the park was extended to almost its present size. James V was succeeded by his daughter, Mary, born a week before his death in 1542. Mary Stuart arrived at Leith from France, at the age of eighteen, on 19 August 1561. The skies were dark, there was a sea fog, her arrival was unexpected and no welcome awaited her. In due course some wretched ponies appeared, to convey her and her baggage to Holyrood, but she is said to have wept at this reception, after leaving the comforts and splendour of the French court to which she was used. However, bonfires were lit and in the early hours of the following morning Queen Mary was awoken at Holyroodhouse by 'most honest men' making music with a three-stringed fiddle outside her window, perhaps not so different from the bagpipes which greet the modern visitor to the palace when the Court is in residence. This is not the place to tell again the story of the tragic life of Mary, Queen of Scots; the 'divers discord and jars' of her disastrous married life with Henry Stewart, Lord Darnley, whom she described as 'the properest and best proportioned long man that ever I saw'; the murder of David Rizzio, while the Queen was at supper; Darnley's own murder as he lay, with smallpox, at Kirk of Field; and Queen Mary's subsequent marriage a few months later to the divorced Earl of Bothwell.

Mary's son, James VI and I, went south to rule the new united kingdom and the palace went through one of its periods of neglect. For the coronation of Charles I at Holyrood in 1633 extensive repairs had to be undertaken in the abbey church. An attempt was made to clean up the filthy streets of the town and the heads of malefactors, spiked on the city gates, were removed. Used as a barracks during the Protectorate, an accidental fire did much damage, but James V's tower survived and repairs were undertaken on Oliver Cromwell's orders.

In 1660, at the Restoration of Charles II, Holyrood again became a palace and the official royal residence in Scotland. The Duke of Lauderdale, the ruthless Secretary of State for Scotland, was effectively ruler of the country under the King. As Commissioner to Parliament he took up residence at Holyrood and with Sir William Bruce, Surveyor-General and Overseer of the King's Buildings in Scotland, he devised a scheme to transform the old-fashioned tower building into a modern palace; a symbol of the King's power in his Scottish kingdom. Money was voted by the Privy Council and by July 1671 work was begun on a reconstruction of the main quadrangle of the palace. The old north-west tower was balanced by a new south-west one in similar late Gothic style, a scheme already contemplated by Charles I. This was to be linked by a formal range of apartments, with a reconstruction of the other three sides of the quadrangle behind. Above the entrance doorway was set a splendid coat-of-arms, surmounted by a magnificent crown and device. Both on this front, and in the orders of pilasters on the east front and in the central courtyard, there is considerable French influence in the architecture. The work was, however, never completed, partly because Charles II lost interest in the project and never visited his magnificent new palace. Sir William Bruce was dismissed in 1678 on the grounds that the work was by then virtually complete, which was not the case. The Duke of York, the King's brother, stayed there several times as Lord High Commissioner and fitted up the Council Chamber as a Catholic chapel. In 1687, as James VII and II, he made a Chapel Royal in the abbey buildings 'to the end that Catholic worship may with the more decency and security be exercised at Edinburgh'. This so angered the Scots that, in the revolution the following year, the mob ransacked the chapels and even broke into the royal vault and tore open the royal lead coffins.

A further long period of neglect fell upon the palace. Succeeding monarchs never visited their northern kingdom. William Adam, as Clerk and Storekeeper of the Works in Scotland, when asked in 1733 to report to the Government on the condition of the buildings, stated that £4,000 needed to be spent on repairs to the roof. Only £3,000 was forthcoming. Various apartments in the palace were occupied by Scottish nobles by virtue of their offices, but the royal Great Apartment was empty. It was described by John Wesley in 1780 as 'dirty as stables'. In 1745 Prince Charles Edward, the 'Young Pretender', had stayed at Holyrood, but he had used the Duke of Hamilton's rooms.

At the end of the century the Comte d'Artois, brother of Louis XVI, was allowed to use the palace with other members of the French Royal Family after they had fled from France in the Revolution, and in 1831, after seven years on the French throne as Charles X, he returned in exile to Holyrood.

When George IV visited Edinburgh in 1822 he was the first reigning monarch to visit Scotland since Charles II, and his arrival caused tumultous excitement. He actually stayed at Dalkeith House, but he held levées, courts and drawing-rooms at the palace and before leaving Scotland he commissioned repairs to the building. All the arrangements

for his visit were masterminded by Sir Walter Scott, and the Hanoverian King appeared wearing full Highland dress, a costume emulated by his Scottish subjects.

In 1833 it was decided that the Lord High Commissioner to the Church of Scotland, the Sovereign's representative at the General Assembly, should use the Great Apartment of the palace while the Assembly was sitting: a tradition which has continued to this day.

On her first visit to Scotland in 1842, Queen Victoria stayed outside Edinburgh as there was a case of scarlet fever at Holyrood. In late August 1850 she travelled north to Balmoral Castle by train, stayed at the palace for the first time and subsequently returned each autumn, up to 1861, for short visits on journeys to and from Aberdeenshire. The Queen was fascinated by the history of 'this old pile, which has seen many deeds more bad, I fear, than good', although her Foreign Secretary, Lord Clarendon, told his wife that the palace was 'a ramshackle sort of place – ugly, dreary and cold'. The royal party used the Great Apartment on the first floor of the palace, which had never been used by a British sovereign since the rooms had been decorated for Charles II. Robert Matheson, architect of the Office of Works in Scotland, managed, on a small budget, rapidly to decorate and furnish the suite. In the 1850s the exterior of the palace was also refurbished. A new carriage drive made it possible to approach the palace down Abbey Hill from the north, instead of from the Royal Mile; the gardens were enlarged in 1857 and in the 1860s a new guardroom and stables replaced a brewery. The fountain in the Outer Courtyard was put up in 1861 at the request of Queen Victoria, in place of a statue of herself. Based on the design of the fountain of 1628 at Linlithgow Palace, it was by Matheson, but included small historical figures designed by Charles Doyle and carved by John Thomas. From 1854 the Historical Apartments were regularly open to the public and in 1872, on her first visit to Holyrood after the death of the Prince Consort, Queen Victoria made a careful tour of much of the 'old, gloomy, but historical Palace'. On this occasion she used a different and prettier suite of rooms, but her later visits were infrequent.

In the reign of King George V the Palace of Holyroodhouse, after so many years as the poor relation among royal residences, at last became a family home. Queen Mary took the palace to her heart as no other member of the Royal Family had ever done. She organized extensive alterations and improvements to the interior and set about completing parts of the decoration left unfinished in the reign of Charles II. She unearthed eighteenth-century furniture, long stored away but never actually disposed of. In 1920-22 gate piers and wrought iron screens were erected in the courtyard as the Scottish National Memorial to Edward VII. Since this period the Palace of Holyroodhouse has been regularly used as a royal residence. The summer visit of Her Majesty Queen Elizabeth II for investitures, garden parties and other events is a keenly awaited moment in the Scottish calendar.

In 1771 Tobias Smollett, in *Humphry Clinker*, described the palace as 'an elegant piece of architecture, but sunk in an obscure, and, as I take it, unwholesome bottom, where one would imagine it had been placed on purpose to be concealed'. Today the old brewery no longer stands near the entrance gates; the air of the city is clean; and the palace, beautifully cared for and in excellent condition, gives a sparkling welcome to the Queen and her guests on her annual visits, and to tourists from all over the world who flock to this ancient centre of Scottish history.

Illustrations

The clock tower over the main entrance (left).

The east front.

The abbey church of Holyrood, with Salisbury Crags in the distance.

The Edward VII Memorial Gates.

The west front of the abbey church.

The abbey church with Arthur's Seat in the distance.

The stone fountain in the Outer Court.

A lamp in the Outer Court.

The memorial to Edward VII, unveiled by King George V in 1922.

The west front of Holyroodhouse.

The North Prospect of Windsor Castle, *painted in oils by Leonard Knyff early in the reign of Queen Anne.*

WINDSOR CASTLE

•

*Situated just over twenty miles west of London, Windsor Castle is the
largest inhabited castle in the world. The oldest royal residence still in use,
it is the home of Her Majesty Queen Elizabeth II, 900 years after its
founder, William the Conqueror, began to build it.*

'The most beautiful, and most pleasantly situated Castle, and Royal Palace, in the whole Isle of Britain', as Daniel Defoe described it, Windsor Castle is known to every tourist who visits this country, and is seen to great advantage by those who arrive by air at Heathrow, as their planes circle almost perilously close to the great Norman building with its amazing skyline, the envy of any film-set designer, its towers, battlements and solid stone. This symbol of our heritage, with its great feeling of antiquity, retains, with its sparkling, well-kept appearance, the vitality of a pleasant and cheerful residence. The Round Tower, the ancient keep on its motte, surrounded now by the beautifully cared-for and brilliantly flowering moat gardens, symbolizes the marriage of the old with the excellence of the new.

The original castle was built, after the Norman Conquest of 1066, as one of a series of fortresses designed to control the approaches to London, on its commanding position overlooking the Thames. 'William the Conqueror did pitch upon it as a pleasant Situation, in a delightful sporting Country, and agreeable to him, who delighted much in Hunting.' Succeeding monarchs left their mark on its structure. Only forty years after the Conquest Henry I held his court there, and Henry II replaced much of the original timber buildings with stone. Edward III took 'an extreme Liking to the Place, because of its beautiful Situation, and pleasing Prospect, which, indeed, is not to be out-done in any Part of the Kingdom', and in 1348 he founded there his new order of chivalry, the Order of the Garter. He reconstructed an earlier chapel built by Henry III, and dedicated it to St George. He also built St George's Hall and rebuilt Henry II's royal apartments. Masons and carpenters from all over the country came to Windsor to carry out the work, stone was brought from many quarries, and four woods were felled for use in the great project.

The chapel, which later fell into disrepair, was rebuilt in 1475 by Edward IV in magnificent Perpendicular style, and completed by Henry VII and Henry VIII. Queen Mary I built lodgings for distinguished retired soldiers, opposite the chapel, to house the Poor Knights, later known as the Military Knights. Queen Elizabeth added a Long Gallery on the north front, and a new chapel. She laid out the North Terrace where, according to Defoe, she 'walked for an Hour every Day before her Dinner, if not hindered by windy Weather, which she had a peculiar Aversion to'. If wet, 'she rather loved to walk in a mild, calm Rain, with an Umbrella over her Head', and look down upon 'Part of the finest, and richest, Vale in the World' with the Thames 'gliding gently through the Middle of it, and inriching by its Navigation, both the Land and the People on every Side'.

During the Civil War the castle was occupied by Parliamentary forces, many of the treasures of St George's Chapel were destroyed, and the forests were devastated. At the Restoration, Charles II, finding the castle, in John Evelyn's words, 'exceedingly ragged and ruinous', decided to emulate his cousin, Louis XIV, at Versailles. He employed the architect Hugh May to convert it into what Celia Fiennes, in 1698, described as 'the finest pallace the king has'. Gazing down from the Round Tower, 'the tower on the leads' as she called it, she also admired the 'great prospect of the whole town and Winsor Forrest, the country round to Kensington'. The castle, this 'Place fitted for the Entertainment of Kings', has fascinated and intrigued artists down the centuries, from Van der Wyngerde in the fifteenth century to John Piper in the reign of King George VI, but it was Paul Sandby, in the later part of the eighteenth century, who most vividly illustrated the castle and its precincts.

Windsor was neglected in the early Hanoverian period, but George III loved it and took a great interest in the surrounding farms. He commissioned James Wyatt to Gothicize Charles II's Baroque interiors, in keeping with his idea of a castle, but in 1805 Queen Charlotte was sorry to move from the Queen's Lodge, a 'neat little seat' opposite the south front of the castle, into 'the coldest house, rooms and passages that ever existed'. Suffering from the distressing disease porphyria, George III lived for the last ten years of his life in a suite of rooms overlooking the North Terrace. His equestrian statue in the Great Park, known as the Copper Horse, closes the three-mile-long vista at the end of the Long Walk, 'of a huge length into the Forrest, which King Charles made for his going out in divertion of shooteing', in the words of Celia Fiennes.

The Great and Little Parks had provided splendid hunting for successive kings. 'Thy Forests, *Windsor!* and thy green Retreats, At once the Monarch's and the Muse's Seats', as Alexander Pope wrote, in his *Windsor-Forest,* in 1704:

Here Hills and Vales, the Woodland and the Plain,
Here Earth and Water seem to strive again,
Not *Chaos*-like together crush'd and bruis'd,
But as the World, harmoniously confus'd:
Where Order in Variety we see …

When George III came to the throne in 1760 the Great Park, an area extending to some 4,500 acres, was mainly rough woodland and swamp, although in 1730 John Loveday of Caversham wrote of the 'Ridings in Windsor Forest' where soldiers had just completed 'clearing the

Ground of Fern &c' for the Royal Family's hunting. George III drained, cleared and reclaimed parts of the Park as farmland, and his uncle, William, and his brother, Henry, successive Dukes of Cumberland and both Rangers of the Great Park, landscaped areas of the park, including Virginia Water. The elder Duke also cut out many grass rides and glades and planted sweet chestnut, Scots pine and beech trees, some of which survive. Much of the Great Park is, as in Defoe's day, still open for 'taking the Air for any Gentlemen that please'.

It is to George IV, that most extravagant of monarchs, that we owe the present romantic appearance of the castle itself. He employed the architect Jeffry Wyatville to double the height of the Round Tower, thereby creating the dramatic silhouette. He also transformed the interior, which has remained to a great extent unaltered to the present day, and laid out the formal garden on the east front. His designs were on a lavish scale, but he died before they were completed, and his brother, William IV, moved into the castle.

The young Queen Victoria enjoyed Windsor Castle as a pleasant country residence in the early married years of her reign, before she and Prince Albert acquired their retreats on the Isle of Wight and Deeside. They developed the Slopes, with a carriage road through them, planted many trees, and laid out Pleasure Grounds on the east front, which the Queen felt would 'make Windsor most agreeable & we shall feel that it is *our* creation'. However, public access to the Home Park made privacy almost impossible, and the Queen had to walk through the 'mob', to escape on to the 'newly-enclosed lawn, with many admirable broad gravel walks'. Roads were finally moved in order to keep the public out of the Home Park.

Near the Pleasure Grounds the Queen and Prince Albert made a skittle ground, and built kennels, an aviary and a poultry farm. The Prince developed the farms on the estate, using new, and in some cases, revolutionary, methods. The Royal Dairy at Frogmore, for instance, built in 1858, combined patronage of architects and sculptors to make it a 'perfect gem of taste and art', with the most hygienic and up-to-date methods of handling milk and milk products, before the use of refrigeration. After the death of her beloved Prince, Queen Victoria spent much of her time at Windsor planning and supervising the building of the Royal Mausoleum at Frogmore.

During the later nineteenth century further alterations were made to the castle buildings: the Horseshoe Cloisters, for instance, originally built in about 1480 to house the Priest Vicars, were restored by Giles Gilbert Scott, and the silhouette of the thirteenth century Curfew Tower was transformed by Anthony Salvin and given a Germanic roofline approved by the Prince Consort.

With the accession of King Edward VII, everything changed. The interior of the castle was modernized for the parties which now took place. During his brief reign King Edward VIII spent little time at the castle, preferring the informality of Fort Belvedere in the Great Park, where he had lived before his accession. He laid out and levelled ground at Smith's Lawn for a small aerodrome, now the polo ground.

Royal Lodge, in Windsor Great Park, near Cumberland Lodge, was given to King George VI, and with Queen Elizabeth he created a beautiful woodland garden there. In 1932 Eric Savill became Deputy Surveyor of Windsor Great Park, and, with inspiration and tireless energy, he began to lay out the Savill Gardens, named after him at the wish of King George VI. Seeing the gardens in their early days, King George V and Queen Mary are said to have remarked: 'It is very small, Mr Savill, but very nice.' King George VI and Queen Elizabeth encouraged and exchanged ideas with him. At first, although it was open to the public, few people knew of this magic garden, but today a large number of visitors enjoy the delights which it has to offer, with its vistas of beautiful planting and specialized botanical species, in a setting of great forest trees, skilfully trimmed to give shade or shelter to smaller plants.

In 1947, with the support of King George VI, another garden was created in the area near Virginia Water, lying south of the Savill Gardens. Rides were laid out, some old trees were removed, and others were pruned.

Over the last thirty years the activities at Windsor have increased in many ways. Her Majesty The Queen has her own private garden, tucked away under the south wall of the castle, and can enjoy her family, her dogs, and her riding; although so near London, she can escape the public eye, if not the noise of jet aircraft. His Royal Highness Prince Philip has developed and enjoyed carriage driving, and there are shooting, polo and endless activities for younger members of the family.

Ceremonial occasions, such as State visits, or those relating to the Order of the Garter, take place at Windsor as they have always done. On a public occasion like the Royal Windsor Horse Show, floodlighting or a firework display accents the amazing silhouette of this most venerable agglomeration of buildings. Windsor Castle seems 'by Nature, to be formed for a Palace; and for Delight; all Kinds of Pleasure and Convenience, that any Country, at least in *England*, can afford, are to be found here'.

Illustrations

The east front of Buckingham Palace, *painted in watercolour by Joseph Nash in 1848,*
showing the Marble Arch in its original position.

BUCKINGHAM PALACE

•

The great ceremonial centre of the country and the Commonwealth, from
which Her Majesty The Queen reigns, Buckingham Palace is a symbol of the
continuity of the British monarchy. Standing as it does in the very centre of
London, it is seen by every visitor to the capital.

Whenever Her Majesty The Queen is in residence, the Royal Standard can be seen flying from the flagstaff on the roof of Buckingham Palace. The palace is the symbol of State and Commonwealth, and from it the Sovereign carries out her public duties as constitutional monarch. In the 600 rooms inside the palace the official business is done, but it is also a private home and, despite its position in the centre of a great capital city, it is unique among palaces in its position facing a park, having a large garden with lake and lawns, and thereby retaining something of the flavour of a country house.

Of all the royal residences in this country Buckingham Palace is the most palatial, but, with constant additions and alterations, it has grown from a large town house built at the end of the seventeenth century by the Duke of Buckingham. As Buckingham House it was acquired by George III in 1762 as a dower house for his consort, Queen Charlotte. They liked it so much that they used it as their London home, and many of their thirteen children were born there. When George IV came to the throne he abandoned Carlton House, his own magnificent creation, and commissioned the architect John Nash to remodel Buckingham House for his use. As at Windsor Castle, George IV, having spent enormous sums of money on the project, never lived to see his grand schemes completed; his brother, William IV, disliked the house and never lived there.

On succeeding her uncle, Queen Victoria instantly moved into the new palace from Kensington Palace, where she had been born and was living with her mother. She found the rooms charming and comfortable: 'I delight in Buckingham Palace,' she told her half-sister. Soon after her marriage Queen Victoria converted one of the Nash conservatories, which projected into the garden, into a private chapel. This remained in use until it was bombed in the Second World War, and, mainly at the suggestion of His Royal Highness Prince Philip, was rebuilt twenty-six years ago as the Queen's Gallery, where pictures and works of art from the Royal Collection are shown in a series of exhibitions, enabling the general public to see many royal possessions not normally on display.

Queen Victoria moved into a palace which was built round three sides of a central courtyard. Following her marriage and the rapid increase in numbers of her children, it became much too small for 'our little family which is fast growing up', so she and Prince Albert decided to employ Edward Blore to close in the fourth side of the Nash quadrangle. This was completed by 1850 and in the following year the Marble Arch, which formerly stood outside the palace, was moved to its present position near Cumberland Gate. The closing façade, architecturally undistinguished, was accused by a rival architect, Thomas Cubitt, of being 'little more than an ordinary piece of street architecture', but it contained rooms for the children, their servants, and household offices. At Prince Albert's suggestion, Blore incorporated the balcony in the centre of the east front, which at once became the focal point of the building and remains an important centrepiece on all ceremonial occasions.

The problem of space inside the palace was solved for only a short time. By the mid-1850s it was decided to build a ballroom and other State rooms on the south side of the palace, and James Pennethorne was chosen as architect. The new suite of rooms enabled the Queen and her successors to entertain enormous numbers of guests. For events such as investitures, and the annual evening reception for members of the diplomatic corps in London, there is ample space for the guests to walk about and enjoy at leisure the treasures which the palace contains.

The Blore east front weathered badly, and in 1913 the architect Sir Aston Webb was called upon to re-case it with the now familiar façade. King George V stipulated that the job was to be completed within four months, so 350 men worked at it by day and 180, by the light of flares, worked at night. When the operation was successfully finished on time, a dinner was given for all the workmen involved. So skilfully was the work carried out that none of the glass in the windows was moved, although the surface of the front was completely altered and its appearance transformed.

When Queen Victoria first moved into her palace in 1837, before the courtyard was closed in, the view to the west, towards St Paul's Cathedral, was a peaceful one. Her children's governess, Lady Lyttelton, wrote: 'I enjoy my quiet here a good deal. No sound but a very distant roar of carriages, that one might take for a waterfall; and bleating of sheep in the Green Park, and screaming of peacocks in the garden, and very often a chorus of nightingales from the high trees.' After the Queen's death all this was transformed. The Queen Victoria Memorial, by Sir Thomas Brock, was set up in 1911, with an architectural surround by Webb, who also designed the new layout of the roads in front of the palace. At first it was planned to have shrubs in the flower beds surrounding the memorial, but Queen Mary was anxious that the beds should be planted with bright flowers and this suggestion has been followed ever since. The intimate impression of the 1830s had finally gone for ever, and, set in the centre of a great metropolis, Buckingham Palace had at last become a palace rather than an overgrown country house.

To the south-west of the palace lie the Royal Mews. For many centuries the 'King's Mewse', or place where the King's falcons were kept, was on the site of the present Trafalgar Square. Following a fire at the royal stables, which was formerly near the present Bloomsbury, the horses were brought to Charing Cross. When George III acquired Buckingham House, he used these stables as well as the existing ones at his new house. In 1764 John Nash built for him the present Riding School. In the next reign Nash was employed by George IV to re-design completely the stables and coach house. In the new quadrangle, entered through an archway from Buckingham Palace Road, the state coaches occupied the east side. There were stables on the west and north sides, with accommodation above for grooms, coachmen and chauffeurs. The gardens of the palace were originally landscaped by W.T. Aiton. After her marriage Queen Victoria and Prince Albert took an increasing interest in them. They enjoyed the peace that could be found there, with birds singing, flowering shrubs and the smell of the lime trees. They made a considerable collection of various wild fowl, gold and silver pheasants and rare aquatic species. Duck houses were provided for these, and the Prince taught them to come to him when he whistled and fed them from a small bridge leading to the island on the lake.

In 1842 Queen Victoria and Prince Albert decided to build a

cottage ornée, or 'a place of Refuge' in the south corner of the gardens, and have it decorated in fresco by various artists, including Sir Edwin Landseer. Prince Albert was closely involved with the scheme for painting scenes on the walls of the new Houses of Parliament in fresco, a technique redeveloped in Germany; the Garden Pavilion formed part of the experiment. There are constant references in the Queen's Journal to visits to the building to watch the artists at work. The pavilion was completed by 1845, but unfortunately the walls later deteriorated through damp and the building was demolished in 1928.

On 28 June 1897, as part of the celebrations for the Diamond Jubilee of Queen Victoria, a garden party was held in the grounds of the palace and visitors from all over the British Empire were present. One of the attractions for guests was to be rowed on the lake by the Queen's Watermen. The garden party tradition developed, and today Her Majesty The Queen holds three parties each summer for guests from all over this country and the Commonwealth. On each occasion 8,000 guests are invited to walk through the palace and out on to the camomile lawns. There they can enjoy the music of two military bands, an excellent tea, and a wander round the beautifully manicured gardens or the more rustic area by the lake, and catch glimpses of members of the Royal Family who attend the event.

Illustrations

Buckingham Palace, seen across the lake in St James's Park (left).

The east front and the Victoria Memorial.

The garden front.

View in the gardens showing the Wellington Vase, originally ordered in Tuscany by Napoleon, and presented to George IV after the battle of Waterloo.

The Admiralty Temple, thought to have been designed by William Kent.

The Royal Mews.

View across the lake in the gardens.

The garden front, seen from the island.

The entrance gates, designed by Aston Webb.

Sunset across the lake.

The Victoria Memorial.

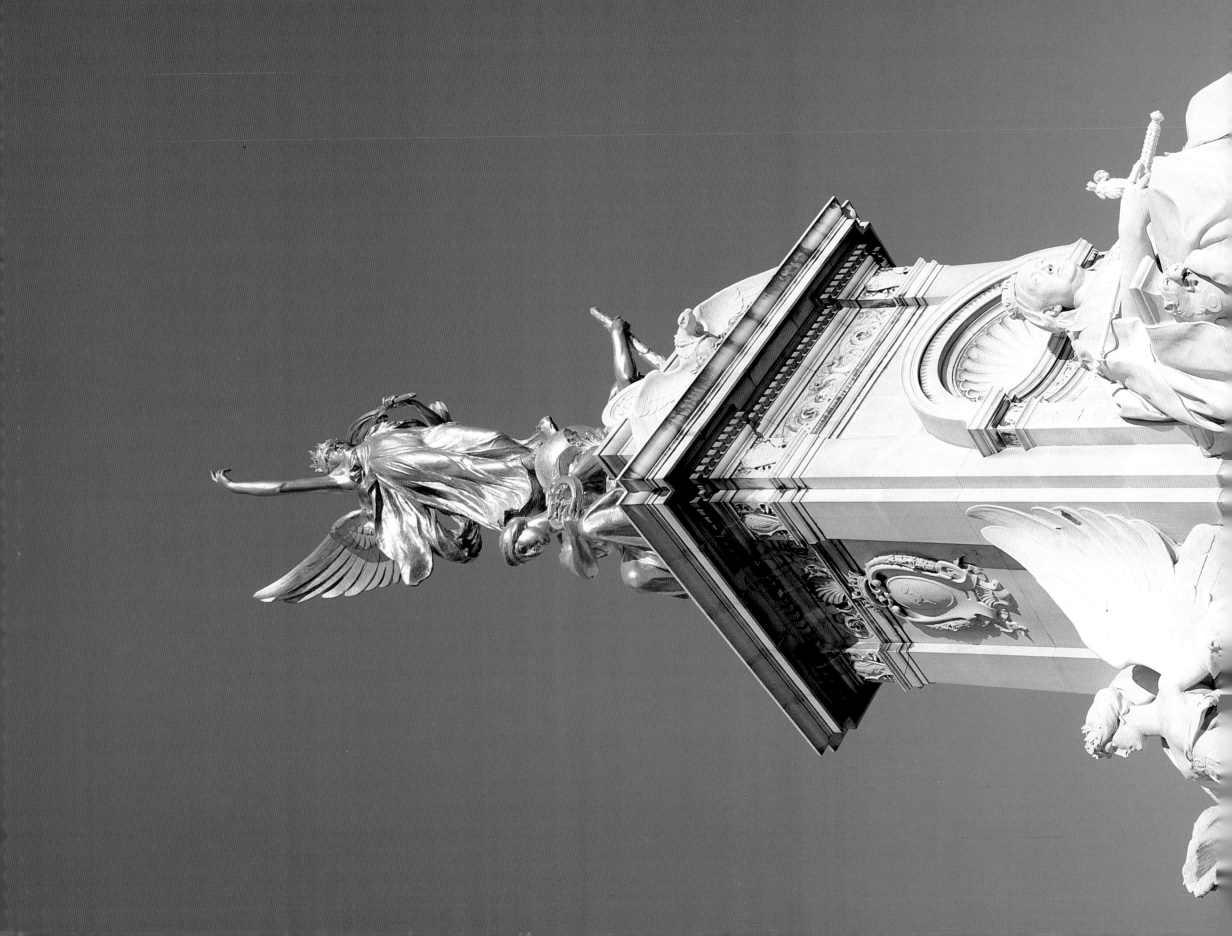

The Old and New Castles at Balmoral, *painted in watercolour for Queen Victoria by Colebrooke Stockdale in 1856.*

BALMORAL CASTLE

The Balmoral estate on Deeside, eight miles west of Ballater, was acquired by Prince Albert and Queen Victoria 150 years ago. The existing shooting-box was replaced by a baronial castle built of Aberdeenshire granite. It has remained a place where the Royal Family can relax in the splendid countryside and enjoy their sporting interests.

Queen Victoria and Prince Albert visited Scotland three times in the early 1840s. They were delighted by the beauty of the countryside and much liked the people. After an exceptionally wet visit in 1847 to Loch Laggan near the west coast, they had the opportunity, for their next visit to the northern kingdom, of renting a small castle or shooting-box in Aberdeenshire. They were assured by the royal physician that the dry air of Deeside would be particularly good for them and for their children and so, from the autumn of 1848, they began to visit Balmoral Castle for several weeks each year. Extra staff quarters had to be built as well as a temporary ballroom in order to accommodate their large party, but in 1852 it became possible to purchase the fee simple of the estate in Prince Albert's name. The Prince, with his architect William Smith of Aberdeen, at once began to design a new castle. The increasing number of royal children – three were born between 1848 and 1853, adding to the five already in the nursery – necessitated more rooms and a larger staff.

The foundation stone of the new castle was laid on 28 September 1853, although by this time the first storey of the house was already partly built. The watercolour by Colebrooke Stockdale shows a unique view of both castles in 1856, just before the demolition of the old one, seen on the left, and before the new one, which stands nearer to the River Dee and commands better views, was completed. A plaque marking the site of the old house can still be seen sunk into the lawn on the garden side of the new house. Queen Victoria was infinitely proud that the Prince was largely responsible for the new castle: '… *all* has become my dearest Albert's *own* creation, own work, own building, own laying out.' *The Times* described the building as 'of the Scotch baronial style of architecture, modified in some details, so as to combine the more bold and prominent features of the ancient stronghold with the more domestic character of modern civilization'.

Prince Albert embarked on an extensive tree-planting campaign, and, as a result of this, the castle is now sheltered and cannot be seen from all sides as was originally the case. Occasional storms have destroyed some of the trees, but a constant replanting programme, which would have won the approval of the Prince, has been carried out on the estate. He and Queen Victoria suffered from the lack of privacy, and in 1857 the main south Deeside road from Ballater to the old Bridge of Dee at Invercauld, near Braemar, was diverted across the river to the northern side, away from the castle. Queen Victoria was later to decide that the railway line from Aberdeen, which ran as far west as Ballater, should not be continued to Braemar. Ballater station has now been closed for some years and visitors must travel to 'Royal Deeside' by car or coach.

Upon their arrival at Balmoral Queen Victoria and Prince Albert at once became closely involved with the welfare of their tenants on their new estate. Inevitably the royal visits provided more work. Living conditions were improved, cottages were renovated and others were built. A school and a library were established by the royal landlords. The tradition of care for the tenants has been carried on ever since, and excellent cottages have recently been built at Easter Balmoral.

On the nine-hole golf course near the castle, facing each other across the first fairway, stand full-length statues of Queen Victoria and the Prince Consort. The statue of the Prince, wearing Highland dress and the Order of the Garter, was erected in 1868. It is a monumental replica in bronze of a marble statue by William Theed inside the castle, which was made in 1862. Queen Victoria superintended every stage of its making, anxious to guarantee an authentic likeness of her beloved Prince, and finally decided that it was the best sculptural image of him: 'beautiful, and so like'. As her preferred likeness of the Prince, a version of it was set up in the market place of his home town of Coburg, and another was sent to Sydney, New South Wales. The statue of the Queen was put up in 1887 to commemorate her Golden Jubilee.

Prince Albert designed a new dairy, completed only after his death, which was in constant use until the Ayrshire dairy herd was finally sold in 1965. Later generations of royal landlords have continued to take an interest in the farms on the estate, as he did. Recently the dairy cattle were replaced by three beef herds. In 1955 Highland cattle were introduced to the estate; in 1966 Luing cattle, a breed of Highland cattle crossed with Shorthorns, were added; and finally, in 1972, a herd of Galloways was acquired.

The forests, originally planted by Prince Albert, have grown to maturity. Where necessary, the trees have been replaced with those from nurseries on the estate, which were also used to fill the gaps left by the great gale in the area in 1953. The Ballochbuie Forest, which adjoined the Balmoral estate, was one of the last remaining Caledonian pine forests. Already in the early 1840s a contemporary guide book mourned the felling there of old trees, sixty feet tall and up to fourteen feet in girth. The forest was acquired by Queen Victoria in 1878 in order to prevent it being totally cut down by the neighbouring landlord. In recent years parts of it have been fenced off to allow it to regenerate, as this had become impossible due to the ravages of grazing deer.

Over the years a good relationship has been maintained with mountain and climbing clubs, to facilitate expeditions up Lochnagar, the mountain which lies on the Balmoral estate and which was described by Queen Victoria as 'the jewel of all the mountains here'. The Glen Muick and Lochnagar Wildlife Reserve helps to educate and assist visitors who wish to study the prolific and important wildlife of the area.

In the fourteen years from 1848 until the death of the Prince, Queen Victoria and her family spent up to six weeks at Balmoral each year. In her widowhood, the Queen spent more time there, often going north for some weeks in early summer, as well as in the late summer and autumn. In the course of her life she spent over 4,000 nights at the castle. On her death King Edward VII succeeded to the property and it was left in turn to each of his successors. He spent less than a month there each year, but King George V, his son and his granddaughter have usually visited Balmoral for about two months each autumn.

It was the sport of shooting deer which most appealed to Prince Albert, and Queen Victoria rejoiced when she was able to report that he had killed among 'the finest, largest stags in the whole neighbourhood – or indeed in almost any forest'. Edward VII, as Prince of Wales, enjoyed the stalking, as did King George V, who was one of the best shots in the country. King George also enjoyed the fishing. There was salmon or trout fishing in Loch Muick, and in recent years the fishing on the Dee has been particularly enjoyed by Her Majesty Queen Elizabeth, The Queen Mother. There was little grouse-driving on the estate in the reign of his father, but King George VI was able to lease some of the best moors in Scotland on nearby estates and develop this sport. The gathering together of the party for luncheon, with the ladies, the picnic baskets and the plaid rugs, would have appealed to Queen Victoria, who enjoyed sitting out on the hillside

sketching with her Ladies in Waiting. Queen Victoria's first attempts at gardening at Balmoral were made difficult, especially where growing vegetables was concerned, by the number of rabbits; but her Lady in Waiting, Lady Canning, noted in August 1849 that the garden was 'in great beauty, all the summer roses in full bloom & the strawberries, gooseberries & currants just ripening'. Queen Mary, after the First World War, laid out elaborate flower gardens at Balmoral, and the rose garden which bears her name. Today there are greenhouses and a large kitchen garden.

Each generation has found pleasure and enjoyment in the life at Balmoral, the beauty of the countryside, with the clear, clean air of the mountains, and the unspoilt landscape, with its absolute peace. The sudden surprises of beautiful natural phenomena: standing on the bridge over the Garbh-Allt Falls watching the stream rushing down and whirling round the rocks after a particularly heavy storm, or the sparkling light of the sun catching the snowy tips of Queen Victoria's favourite mountain, Lochnagar. A hundred and fifty years ago tourists already presented problems. It is, however, still possible to escape from the noise and confusion of modern living in large stretches of the Balmoral estate. The crowds which gathered round Queen Victoria at the Braemar Gatherings, or watched her arrive to attend services at Crathie church were, however, small compared to those who turn out to see her successors.

For Queen Victoria much of the pleasure of Balmoral involved the simple things denied to a reigning Queen in the south. She loved to visit the old ladies on the estate and take tea and scones with them. Not so very much has changed in the Balmoral of the 1990s and, if it is not the same family who keep the village shop in Easter Balmoral, at least the same welcoming, friendly atmosphere would greet a royal visitor as when, in 1850, Queen Victoria sat down to make her sketches of little Mary Symons, the merchant's daughter.

Illustrations

Photograph of old Sandringham House in 1864.

SANDRINGHAM HOUSE

●

*The most recently acquired of the Queen's residences, Sandringham House
is near the historic town of King's Lynn in Norfolk. It has been the private
country home of four generations of sovereigns. Much loved by its owners,
the grounds are beautiful and the surrounding country perfect for sport.*

'Dear old Sandringham, the place I love better than anywhere else in the world.' King George V's words sum up much of the feeling of members of the Royal Family about this large, ugly, red-brick house built in Jacobean style. An eighteenth-century house on the site was acquired in 1862 by the Prince of Wales, later to become Edward VII. After his marriage to Princess Alexandra of Denmark, he realized that he needed much more space for his family, staff and guests, so the house was first altered and finally demolished and rebuilt as we see it today. Park House was also built, near the church, and the Bachelor's Cottage and various lodges. The architect employed was A.J. Humbert, who was working for Queen Victoria on the Royal Mausoleum at Frogmore at the period. The only part of the original house to survive was the conservatory, which was built in the local carrstone and was converted into a billiard room. Eleven years after the house was completed in 1870, a large new ballroom was added. When Constance, Lady Battersea, visited Sandringham in the early 1870s, she wrote that 'although devoid of any historical or architectural interest, it appealed strongly to me through its close connection with the members of the Royal Family, even taking a romantic colouring from the personality of the young and attractive Princess of Wales'. The new house was modern, 'extensive, comfortable, well adapted for entertaining T.R.H.'s numerous and appreciative guests', but in 1891 a fire destroyed a number of rooms on the upper floor, and when the house was repaired more bedrooms were added above the billiard room and bowling alley.

The Prince of Wales's elder son, Albert Victor, Duke of Clarence, died in 1892. He had been engaged to Princess Mary of Teck, who, in the summer of 1893, married instead his younger brother Prince George, later King George V. They were given as their country home the Bachelor's Cottage in the grounds of Sandringham House; it was renamed York Cottage, as the young couple became Duke and Duchess of York. They spent their honeymoon there, arriving after a dusty carriage drive from Wolferton station with the Prince's frockcoat white with dust and the Irish poplin which the bride was wearing a blackish-grey. Queen Victoria thought it an odd choice for a honeymoon spot – 'I regret & think rather *unlucky* & sad' – but the house, now the Sandringham Estate Office, became their much loved home and all their children, with the exception of their eldest, were born there. King George V and his family continued to live in this relatively small house for thirty-three years. 'This house is looking very cosy & nice but it seems smaller than ever!' Queen Mary told her eldest son in 1910, but the family moved into the big house only after the death of Queen Alexandra in 1925. The close proximity of 'Mother dear', the York children's grandmother, could present problems, especially as she considered she understood children better than her daughter-in-law. When the Duke and Duchess of York were abroad on a tour in 1901, Queen Alexandra would drop in at York Cottage to see the children and insist on seeing the youngest baby in its bath. Whether it was bathtime or not, the baby had to be undressed and immersed. At the end of the last century, when bicycling became the rage, the Duke of York and his sisters spent much time at Sandringham riding round the grounds and on wet days were allowed to take refuge and pedal in the ballroom. The Duchess of York rode a tricycle. The modern age was taking over. By the beginning of the new century electricity had replaced gas for lighting the royal homes and telephones had been installed.

Many alterations were made in the gardens when the Prince of Wales acquired the estate. The existing lake was moved, and two further lakes were dug. The elaborate layout, with extensive flower beds in front of the house, has been much modified in recent years. Queen Mary particularly loved herbaceous borders and elaborate bedding-out plants. She owned numbers of contemporary watercolour views of such gardens by artists like Beatrice Parsons, whose work she much admired. Today, the gardens at Sandringham have been much simplified, but are no less beautiful. Beds of flowering shrubs replace more formal planting. The large trees have reached maturity and make a beautiful background to the shrub beds. The handsome wrought-iron gates, known as the Norwich Gates, designed by Thomas Jekyll, which now close the vista of the road from Dersingham, were made for the Great Exhibition of 1862 and given as a wedding present to the Prince and Princess of Wales in the following year by the County of Norfolk and City of Norwich. The North Garden, to the right of the east front, was laid out for King George VI by G. A. Jellicoe, who also laid out the gardens at Royal Lodge. In the centre is a statue of Father Time acquired by Queen Mary in 1950. At the end of the North Garden is a bronze statue of 1690, a joss or idol of the Buddhist god Kuvera, flanked by two Japanese stone animals. The joss was brought from China in 1869 by Admiral Sir Harry Keppel and presented to the Prince of Wales. The Admiral was a close friend of the Royal Family and had already helped the Prince plant the first pear and apple trees in the kitchen gardens at Sandringham. On the arrival of the thirty-hundredweight statue at King's Lynn, it had to be drawn on a carriage, with the entire ship's company pulling the ropes. It took most of a day to reach Sandringham.

On the south wall of the later wing a sundial, placed there when the wing was completed in 1892, is inscribed *'My Time in Thy Hand'* and

'Let others tell of storms and showers I'll only count your sunny hours.' Nearby are the graves of many of Queen Alexandra's dogs. A little summerhouse, known as The Nest, is situated near the rockery by one of the lakes. It was presented to Queen Alexandra in 1913 by General Sir Dighton Probyn, VC, a distinguished soldier who from 1910 was Comptroller of her Household. An inscription on it reads *'The Queen's Nest – A small offering to The Blessed Lady from Her Beloved Majesty's very devoted old servant General Probyn 1913 – Today tomorrow and every day God bless her and guard her I fervently pray.'*

Activities at Sandringham were numerous. Queen Alexandra had sixty dogs in kennels. The Royal pigeon lofts, established in 1886, were even used on active service in the Second World War. Queen Mary set up a carpentry school and wood-carving class for boys on the estate and there were dress-making and needlework classes for the girls.

An extensive stud was developed at Sandringham. The Prince of Wales kept his famous racehorses there: Persimmon who won the Derby, Ascot Gold Cup, Eclipse Stakes and St Leger; Diamond Jubilee, winner of the Derby, Two Thousand Guineas, St Leger and Eclipse Stakes. In the present reign Her Majesty's winning racehorse, Aureole, and her other horses have lived at the Sandringham stud.

The estate at Sandringham has been extended since its acquisition in 1862, and includes land reclaimed from the Wash. Woodlands of up to 2,000 acres are being extensively afforested and this cover makes Sandringham an excellent sporting estate. There are home farms of some 3,000 acres, with beefstock, arable land and fruit farms run on a scientific and economically sound basis, while 15,000 acres is let to tenant farmers. A Country Park with nature trails gives the large visiting public great pleasure and opportunity for recreation.

Many thousands each year also visit the little parish church of St Mary Magdalene at Sandringham and enter by the lychgate through which the Royal Family pass to worship in the church. In the churchyard lie the infant son of King Edward and Queen Alexandra, and Prince John, the fifth son of King George and Queen Mary. The main part of the church dates from the sixteenth century, but it was extensively restored in the nineteenth century and the interior now contains many memorials to members of the Royal Family, especially in the richly decorated chancel and sanctuary.

Although much has been done in recent years to enable the public to see something of the delights which Sandringham has to offer, it remains essentially a family home, where members of the Royal Family can escape the public eye and enjoy the cheerful atmosphere originally created there by one of the most pleasure-loving of our Sovereigns.

Illustrations

The clock tower, erected in memory of Albert Victor, Duke of Clarence and Avondale (left).

Sandringham House, seen from the Upper Lake.

The east front.

The stream near York Cottage.

The north front.

The summerhouse of Edward VII.

The Folly.

The west front.

The pergola in the Walled Garden.

'Father Time.'

Appleton Water Tower, seen across cornfields.

A Bird's Eye View of Hampton Court Palace from the East,
painted in oils by Leonard Knyff in the early eighteenth century.

HAMPTON COURT

•

*Once the home of King Henry VIII, this great Tudor palace stands on the
banks of the River Thames. England's answer to Versailles, it combines its
ancient architecture with the splendid classical buildings of Sir
Christopher Wren. With its beautiful formal gardens the palace, within
reach of London, has given pleasure to generations of visitors.*

Thomas Wolsey, Archbishop of York, acquired a long lease on the manor of Hampton Court from the Knights Hospitallers in 1514. In the following year he became Lord Chancellor of England, was made a cardinal, and became one of the richest and most powerful men in the country. He planned a magnificent palace at Hampton, which was to become a standing monument 'of the excessive Pride, as well as the immense Wealth of that Prelate, who knew no Bounds of his Insolence and Ambition, till he was overthrown at once by the Displeasure of his Master'. Daniel Defoe, writing in the 1720s, considered that Hampton was the finest situation on the river between Staines and Windsor, being 'close to the River, yet not offended by the rising of its Waters in Floods, or Storms, near to the Reflux of the Tides, but not quite so near as to be affected with any Foulness of the Water'. In the brief period in which Cardinal Wolsey lived in great splendour at Hampton Court he had a household of nearly 500, with 200 guest rooms. The poet Skelton wrote sarcastically:

Why come ye not to Court
To whyche Court?
To the Kynges Court,
Or to Hampton Court?
Nay to the Kynges Court:
The Kynges Court
Should have the excellence,
But Hampton Court
Has the preemynence . . .

In 1527 Wolsey fell from favour and handed over Hampton Court, and all its contents, to King Henry VIII. In October 1529 Wolsey's lands and goods were declared forfeit. He was given a general pardon early in 1530, but in November was arrested for high treason and died on the journey to London.

The King set about enlarging Wolsey's great house into one of the most comfortable palaces in the country, and by the time of his death in 1547 it was, apart from Whitehall, the largest Tudor palace. Each of his wives from Anne Boleyn onwards lived there in turn, and Edward VI was born there. The approach to the palace was by river from London: 'as to passing by Water to and from *London*; tho' in Summer 'tis exceeding pleasant, yet the Passage is a little too long to make it easy to the Ladies, especially to be crowded up in the small Boats, which usually go upon the *Thames* for Pleasure'.

The modern approach is by road through George II's Trophy Gates, across Outer Green Court, with the river lying on the right. Ahead lies the west front of the palace, entered, over the remains of the moat, through Wolsey's Great Gatehouse, flanked by projecting wings built by Henry VIII at either end of this front in the mid-1530s. Much of the Tudor brickwork has been re-faced over the years, but the terracotta roundels with heads of Roman emperors, originally coloured and gilded, survive. They were brought here by Henry VIII from the 'Holbein Gate' at the Palace of Whitehall. Through the gatehouse the visitor enters Cardinal Wolsey's Base Court and beyond this, through Anne Boleyn's Gateway, lies Clock Court. Here the gateway is decorated with a further series of terracotta medallions of Roman emperors, modelled by Giovanni da Maiano in 1521 for the Cardinal. The fine terracotta carving of his arms, surmounted by a cardinal's hat, with the date 1525, also survives, restored after being defaced by Henry VIII. The Astronomical Clock, made for the King in 1540 by Nicholas Oursian and much restored in the last century, shows a series of astronomical facts, although, as it was made before the discoveries of Copernicus and Galileo, the sun revolves round the earth. Colour Court was the main courtyard of Wolsey's house, but it has been extensively altered: Henry VIII built the Great Hall on the north side, Wren the colonnade on the south side, and William Kent the apartments on the east side for George II, with the date 1732 carved over the gateway to mark its completion. The clock in this courtyard was sent here by William IV from St James's Palace.

Henry VIII's great new palace required little maintenance during the succeeding reigns. Queen Elizabeth I built a new Privy Kitchen when it was found that the kitchen was beneath her privy closet and that the smell of cooking rose so that she could not 'sytt quiet nor without ill saver'. She also made alterations to the gardens, laid out by her father, between the palace and the river. There were flower beds surrounded by railings painted in the Tudor colours of green and white, and coloured heraldic beasts, five or six feet high, set upon painted posts, each holding metal vanes which revolved in the wind.

According to Defoe, Charles I, who enjoyed 'Country Retirements', 'took great Delight here, and had he liv'd to enjoy it in Peace, had purpos'd to make it another Thing than it was'. He was briefly imprisoned here after the Civil War. Oliver Cromwell used the palace as his country residence during his five years as Protector from the end of 1653.

After the Restoration, Charles II laid out new gardens and made repairs, but it was in the reign of William and Mary that Hampton Court 'put on new Cloaths, and being dress'd gay and glorious, made the Figure we now see it in'. William III and his Queen commissioned Sir Christopher Wren to design a new palace: 'Whoever knew Hampton-Court before it was begun to be. rebuilt, or alter'd, by the late King William, must acknowledge it was a very compleat Palace before, and fit for a King; and tho' it might not, according to the modern Method of Building, or of Gardening, pass for a Thing exquisitely fine; yet it had this remaining to itself, and perhaps peculiar; namely, that it shewed a Situation exceedingly capable of Improvement, and of being made one of the most delightful Palaces in Europe.' A number of designs were produced, including some which involved the destruction of almost the whole Tudor palace, but finally only the third courtyard, Henry VIII's Cloister Green Court with the King's and Queen's Lodgings, was demolished and work was begun in 1689 on the present Fountain Court. This distinguished classical courtyard is approached from Clock Court and around it on the first floor are ranged the two suites of State Rooms, with the King's Side facing south to the Privy Gardens and the Queen's Side looking on to Great Fountain Garden. The brick-built quadrangle of Fountain Court has contrasting Portland stone enrichments. Carved wreaths surround the circular windows on the second storey with, on the south side, in place of windows, painted monochrome panels by Laguerre.

Little of the layout of the earlier gardens remains. Henry VIII's Tiltyard, a seven-acre area enclosed by brick walls, lying to the west of the palace, was turned into kitchen gardens by William and Mary. The Close Tennis Court at the northern end of the east front, usually said to have been built in the reign of Henry VIII, probably dates from early in the reign of Charles I and is still in use. The gardens, replanned in the French style by William and Mary, survive largely unaltered. They were 'designed to be very fine, great fountaines and grass plotts and gravell walks and just against the middle of the house was a very large fountaine and beyond it a large Cannal guarded by rows of even trees that runn a good way'. The gardens at Hampton Court were the only ones laid out in this country by William III, although he was responsible for those at Het Loo and the Huis ten Bosch in Holland. Not as elaborate as the gardens at Versailles, where trees 100 years old were shifted, here the head gardener contrived to move trees thirty years old, and Defoe thought 'the *Wonder* much the less' but 'not the less difficult or nice'. The 'fine Scrolls and Bordure' of the beds laid out in the parterre were edged with box, but, as Queen Mary disliked the smell, these 'Edgings' were removed and only replanted later as being 'so

fair and regular an Edging'.

From Fountain Court, through three elaborate wrought-iron gates, the gardens open out before the visitor. A Broad Walk stretches ahead to the banks of the Thames, nearly half a mile away. Looking back at the long façade of the east front, the middle section, entirely of stone with four Corinthian columns flanking the three windows of the Queen's drawing-room, has a splendid carved centrepiece with drapery, trumpets, crown and sceptre, the initials of William and Mary and a scene in the pediment of Hercules triumphing over Envy, by Caius Cibber.

William III's Orangery, originally planned to have a grotto in the centre, is at ground level on the south side of the palace. His own rooms lay behind it, especially built with low ceilings as he suffered from asthma. Outside it is his Privy Garden: 'private and shady walks, fine aloes, paricantha, mirtles, orranges and oliantas'. On the river bank, at the southern end of the garden, stands Jean Tijou's magnificent wrought-iron screen of the mid-1690s, originally designed for the Great Fountain Garden.

To the west of Tijou's gates, William III converted the Thames Gallery, used 'chiefly for landing from the River', into a Water Gallery for his Queen in 1690. Here she hung the full-length portraits of her court ladies, painted for her by Sir Godfrey Kneller, and kept her fine collection of Chinese porcelain and Delft ware. After her death in 1694 the King was so distressed that he pulled down the little building and erected the present Banqueting House or Pavilion in Glass Case Garden in its place. For some years he also abandoned work on the main palace and withdrew to Kensington. When Celia Fiennes saw Hampton Court in the 1690s, she thought it looked like 'a little town the buildings runn so great a length on the ground, the old buildings and the new part which King William and Queen Mary built; the Queen took great delight in it, the new was but just the shell up and some of the Rooms of State ceil'd but nothing finished.' Although work began again at Hampton Court in 1699, the interiors of the new building were incomplete when William III died in 1702. If he had lived, he would probably have demolished the Tudor palace and rebuilt it in the modern style. He planned the main approach to the palace from the Bushy Park side, with a large forecourt. In 1699 the Bushy Park Avenue was laid out by Henry Wise, the circular basin in the centre, 400 feet across, was dug, and lime and chestnut trees were planted. The handsome Lion Gates, erected opposite the new avenue, bear the monogram of Queen Anne, although set up after her death. The Labyrinth or Maze was planted at this period and the

Wilderness, covering the area between the Lion Gates and the palace, may date from a little earlier.

Antonio Verrio was painting in the interior of the palace during the reign of Queen Anne, and she spent some time at Hampton Court:

Close by those Meads for ever crown'd with Flow'rs,
Where *Thames* with Pride surveys his rising Tow'rs,
There stands a Structure of Majestick Frame,
Which from the neighb'ring *Hampton* takes its Name.
Here *Britain's* Statesmen oft the Fall foredoom
Of Foreign Tyrants, and of Nymphs at home;
Here Thou, Great *Anna!* whom three Realms obey,
Dost sometimes Counsel take – and sometimes *Tea.*
Hither the Heroes and the Nymphs resort,
To taste awhile the Pleasures of a Court;
In various Talk th' instructive hours they past,
Who gave the '*Ball,* or paid the *Visit* last:
One speaks the Glory of the *British Queen,*
And one describes a charming *Indian Screen;*
A third interprets Motions, Looks, and Eyes;
At ev'ry Word a Reputation dies.
Snuff, or the *Fan,* supply each Pause of Chat,
With singing, laughing, ogling, and all that.
(Alexander Pope)

Further decoration of the interior was carried out by George I, who favoured Hampton Court as 'his Choice for the Summer's Retreat of the Court, and where they may best enjoy the Diversions of the Season'. George II was the last Sovereign to carry out building operations there and also the last to live there. George IV went to Hampton Court to visit the royal stud, established there since the reign of William III. In the reign of Queen Victoria the State Apartments were first opened to the public on a regular basis and much maintenance and renovation was carried out.

From the eighteenth century, 'grace-and-favour' apartments, in the gift of the Lord Chamberlain, were granted to the widows of those who had served their country with distinction, and on occasion to others such as the refugee kings William V of Orange and Gustavus IV of Sweden. Charles Dickens took a jaundiced view of the 'dreary red-brick dungeon at Hampton Court', where 'the venerable inhabitants of that venerable pile seemed, in those times, to be encamped there like a sort of civilised gipsies'. He gives an acid description of the world in which these old ladies passed their days. 'Genteel blinds and makeshifts were more or less observable as soon as their doors were opened; screens not half high enough, which made dining-rooms out of arched passages, and warded off obscure corners where footboys slept at night with their heads among the knives and forks; curtains which called upon you to believe that they didn't hide anything; panes of glass which requested you not to see them; many objects of various forms, feigning to have no connection with their guilty secret, a bed; disguised traps in walls, which were clearly coal-cellars; affectations of no thoroughfares, which were evidently doors to little kitchens.' Despite William IV's stricture on the apartments as 'the quality poor house', generations of elderly ladies lived happily there, often with unmarried daughters who enjoyed a cheerful and gregarious social life.

In April 1986 a catastrophic fire was started when an old lady's candle fell over at her bedside in her grace-and-favour apartment. Flames crept behind oak panelling to the State Rooms below. Thanks to the prompt efforts of the volunteer salvage corps almost all the contents were saved, but the cost of the damage amounted to millions of pounds. The restoration, taking over five years, will include replacing sections of limewood carving with copies made from trees planted in 1689 and recently felled in the gardens.

From early in its history Hampton Court has been a favourite place for excursions from London. Its situation, its romance, and the beauty of its setting have invited countless thousands to visit it. A hundred years ago Jerome K. Jerome described the sunny river with the inhabitants of Hampton and Molesey dressed in boating costume, 'dotted and decked with yellow, and blue, and orange, and white, and red, and pink'. When his *Three Men in a Boat* passed the 'mellow, bright, sweet old wall' at Hampton Court, Harris described how he paid his two pence to visit the Maze with a friend who had assured him that 'You keep on taking the first turning to the right. We'll just walk round for ten minutes, and then go and get some lunch.' The problem of reaching the centre of the Maze, and the even greater difficulty in finding the way out ('whatever way they turned brought them back to the middle') has been experienced by visitors of all ages before and since 1889.

Hampton Court is perhaps the most popular royal residence and, despite the crowds attracted on a sunny summer day, the modern visitor might echo Defoe's words: 'I know no Palace in *Europe, Versailles* excepted, which can come up to her, either for Beauty and Magnificence, or for Extent of Building, and the Ornaments attending it.'

Illustrations

The east front and the Fountain Garden.

The west front, showing the entrance to the Lord Chamberlain's Court, the Great Outer Gateway and the Moat Bridge.

The Long Water at sunrise.

'Flower of Spring.'

The Banqueting House and the Pond Garden.

Early morning sunlight on the Banqueting House.

The Tijou gates.

Rooftop detail.

The Queen's Beasts on the Moat Bridge.

Acknowledgements

Many people were involved in the preparation of **The Royal Estates of Britain**, but there are some to whom special thanks must be extended for their advice, help and co-operation, without which the book could not have been produced.

The following reproductions are by gracious permission of Her Majesty The Queen: from the Royal Library, Windsor, the photograph of Sandringham House by Bedford Lemere, *The Old and New Castles at Balmoral* by F. Colebrooke Stockdale, *The Palace of Holyroodhouse by* James Duffield Harding, and *The East Front of Buckingham Palace* by Joseph Nash; from the Royal Collection, *A Bird's Eye View of Hampton Court Palace from the East* and *The North Prospect of Windsor Castle*, both by Leonard Knyff.

We should also like to thank Her Majesty Queen Elizabeth The Queen Mother for granting permission to photograph her private residences, Royal Lodge at Windsor and Birkhall at Balmoral.

Though photographs can tell their own story, the written word is also important and requires a great deal of knowledge and expertise. For this we wish to thank Delia Millar; we thoroughly enjoyed working with her on the book and will always be grateful to her.

Liaison with Buckingham Palace was essential, and our gratitude goes to John Haslam for his co-ordination and direction of this part of the project.

We would also like to thank the many people and companies who gave their invaluable assistance: Lt. Col. Donald Wickes, Mr Martin Leslie, Major Barrie Eastwood, Capt. Roger McClosky, Mr John Bond, Mr Roland Wiseman, Miss Caroline Armitage, Miss Frances Dimond, Mr Julian Loyd, Mr Marcus Bishop, Mr Edward Hewlett, Major Albert Smith, Mr Tom Deighton, Mr John Yarnell, Miss Lindsay Shead; Eleo Gordon, Annie Lee, Joy Harrison, Jan Beesley; Paula Pell-Johnson and Maria Bishop and the rest of the team at Linhof Professional Sales, Joey and Paul Simms of Colourbox and Techunique, Johnsons Photopia (Mamiya), and Elizabeth and Bill Bryce of the Glen Lui Hotel.

Lastly but not least, our love and thanks to our families for their support and encouragement during the production of this book.

Earl A. Beesley
Garry Gibbons